IMMIGRANT

Black Lawrence Press
www.blacklawrence.com

Executive Editor: Diane Goettel
Book Design: Steven Seighman

Black Lawrence Press
115 Center Ave.
Aspinwall, PA 15215
U.S.A.

Author photo by William Wolff
Cover photo, "Orange scrub on one leg," by Doron Hanoch

Published 2010 by Black Lawrence Press, a division of Dzanc Books

First edition 2010
ISBN: 9780982622827

Printed in the United States

IMMIGRANT

poems by
Marcela Sulak

Contents

II. Immigration Quotas

I

The Mouths of the Speechless

Avocado

Wound tight inside the avocado
we once found a perfect copy
of the tree in miniature,
pale, translucent leaves unfurling,
coiled strings of roots, a stem
that split the pit. We didn't have
the heart to toss it out, crowned
with coffee grounds and newspaper.
In the end, the landlady took it
with the rent. She said she'd plant it
among the rocks and jagged shade
against the southern slope for strength
since silky avocado flesh
thrives under adverse conditions.

Falling Fruit

They long to be devoured by a willful traveler
who will rub them soft and let them fall.
They can't wait to go.
                       They bounce in the beds
of cargo trucks, they crowd the sidewalks, they beat
upon the parking lot and streets.
                            In the market they call out
the name of their price. They can always
be talked down. They don't care how many
wrinkled bills you press into the hands
of sweaty women. They don't count the coins
nor admire their portraitures.
                      Sometimes they tear
the shopping bags and dive into the street.
                                Even
the established walnut tree at the Catholic school in Germany
moans all night. We rip the seeds apart in the morning.
Our fingernails are yellow, our tongues
bitter brown.
                At this point Beatriz
pops out the bathroom window. Her hair
is loosened, her shoulders bare
her face is wet. She is smiling shyly.
                          Like this
she is the flesh a mouth would want to hold.
She offers to open the door for me, a foreigner
who has no key. She must have heard
the wooden door. I hadn't called out.
                        Her feet
are printing their wet leaves across the floor.

The Ninth Floor in Caracas

In the streets below Draghitza's body
rain baubles the yellowish-brown light—

her body's wet and slick as street
and brown between the window slats—it's rain-

ing and the pipes groan *porque.*
                      She turns off
the faucet, reaches for the soap, suds

leave her hands and slide the way
stolen bulbs of light slide
                    (on electrical lines

diverted through the mountainside
barrios, where it also rains,

puddling the floor, baby slapping
water and the hair-line cracks of concrete

like the lines around Draghitza's mouth)

                (*I pay for my electricity*
                Franklin says, who lives there).
It's raining

on her bright breasts, it's raining on her belly
down her thighs; the people below are wet

with stolen light.
        No umbrellas
strew their colors —it's too hard

for that—but dogs quiver under lumber
busses splash the same

sloppy syllable across each sidewalk,
the metro opens its mouth, the balcony

becomes a cup.
        The faucet won't turn off. The soap, the soap has
fallen and her body, slick

is shining.
        Draghitza shakes some water
drops from her fingertips, she blurs

in latent steam, is lost in surfeit
sharpens and blurs again.

She has fingerprints and large hands.
She tastes slightly of metal and of sea.

She is always smaller in person
than we expect and more
        than we remember.

The History of the Date

Those aren't wrinkles, merely places where
the skin is burrowing to lick her own
dark sweetness. Since her body's fashioned from
the clay remaining after Adam's spine and hair,
she often yields the fibers of her trees
for baskets, shoes, the rope and needles, thread
her mythic children crafted in their need.
In her youth she tarried near the Euphrates;
Chaldean men en route through Babylon,
Assyrians, caressed and carried her
from one oasis to the next. A year
is worth a date palm, and a month, a frond,
according to the hieroglyphs that suckle
on her absence, spurting syllables.

Jaffa

At the sea we sink our shifting heels
into the sand, examining the seam

where the waves unravel,
where shards of pottery,

shuddered from their historic tables,
sweep themselves along the creaking floor

and tumble to the shore. Once in just this spot
Jonah fell into the belly of a whale.

Who wouldn't like to be the sea sometimes,
it's ambiguous border, its changeful fortresses—

now repelling, now holding close,
slamming the explosive sand

that once joined continents.
This country, for example, breaking

in two. The inhabitants of Jaffa have always hated
what they could not love

and loved what they could not hate.
I'd like to be, just once, a bride,

if only to that old whale,
to set the table with earthenware,

to say something great was holding me here,
this was my provenance—

and someone some day would tell by my shards
where I belonged.

Angels

1.
If the groans and shrieks of martyrs, the shofar cry
of Yom Kippur really rend the heavens, then I picture it
like this: clouds are ripped as if by swords, and angels spill
and spread across the world.

                      Once a rabbi fled from Poland
to the tranquil town of Tzfat, enduring unutterable privations
and fear along the way. As the Galilean hills lift and lull
his tired feet, an angel infestation fills his red, chapped ears.
Their voices chirrup from synagogue

                               to synagogue, he can
almost glimpse their ragged white beneath the turquoise doors,
like lice beneath a skirt of lettuce. And so he leaves for Tiberius
complaining that the angels had kept him up at night.

2.

My grandparents sheltered their hearty human bonds
in a wood-framed rental with a wrap-around porch.
Each of six dark daughters through the years
reduced the sum of chaos by a suitcase as they left.

Though loathe to do it, grandpa dies and leaves
grandma alone. She says she found angels
skittering across soup plates, wrecking havoc
on the crystal. When asked if she would like

to die and join her true love, my grandmother
replies, not unless he stops arguing
with God in the next room. And how
he loves her still, we thought.

3.

The Antimatter of Angels

Antimatter is not found naturally on Earth, except very briefly in small quantities ... because... when matter and antimatter come into contact they annihilate.

Maybe I'm not hurt enough,
or maybe I'm just standing
on the wrong side of eternity.
My only bloodless visitor
comes when I am all alone.
I hope I never know
if his infinity of *no* can really
blot out God the way
he whispers that it can,
just as his colorless shadow
snuffed the closet light
when I was still a child,
how his unbearable approach
silenced my ears; the world
stopped as the windows quaked
against his fingerless whorl.

An Olive, A Letter

Summary of Geneve Fonseca's Inquisition records, Portugal 1642

There are visions that are dangerous:
    purple, blue, or magenta ships
    sailing in a cloudless sky

    your deceased mother
    has taken you to heaven
    your sisters are awaiting
    in the presence of unmarried men

And actions from which you should refrain:
    singing and playing the lute
    taking pleasure with great mirth
    in the making of new clothes

And items that arouse envy or suspicion
    a length of fine green cloth,
    smuggled fishes lightly fried
    a length of purple cloth
    the scent of cinnamon

There are phrases which cannot save you:
    spinning wheel before a window
    famous surgeon husband
    tender age

And if you are shown tokens from heaven
    an ear of corn
    an olive
    a letter
Genevre, give them back.
Genevre, say you're sorry.

The History of Brussel Sprouts

This vegetable evolved from primitive
non-heading Mediterranean kraut.
It wrapped its crinkly little leaves about
its winsome, blooming face and left to live
a classic *Bildungsroman*. Adjusting mien
and flavor, traveling north and west, it came
upon the gates of Brussels, took the name
that welcomed it. Gentlemen and lean
courtesans took into their mouths its tight
green jackets, endlessly disrobing, sheets
of luminosity pressed close. And fleets
dispatched to newer worlds carried wide
and far its seed. Like any immigrant,
it put down roots before it could repent.

Button

My mother kept them in a jar on the windowsill,
next to her Singer sewing machine: moonfaced
with two pairs of eyes, or a single tiny *o* below
each brassy fish, garnet-shaped glass, shades of lilac
never seen in nature, swirls of white and yellow,
mother-of-pearl, taupe, triangular ones and oblong.
I like to think that one day they were scattered
to the seven bolts of fabric in the cabinet,
they married thread and dazzled the eye on various
boulevards. Wherever they are tonight, may they be blessed.
I know for sure whenever something happened to tear apart
what should be joined my mother reached into her jar
and found the missing shape. When something new came
into being we could approximate perfection—
one shade either side of right. These five black buttons
down a chest of gold lame— they are bits of sky
that fell when hungry bulbs of city light chewed
the night like moths on velveteen. They are pools
below the forest, smell like earth in Iowa.
They are the marble countertops of Grecian spas
and midnight in the mausoleum. They are
a lost cause. In my daughter's mouth the first syllable
ascends; the second drops like a toilet seat,
like an acorn, one of those mildly destructive joys
of hers. She is holding the comforter and pulling
at the gaps between the buttons; she tears my sleep
with her little hands, with her six sheathed teeth. Button,
she says, winding her arms around me like a long and sturdy thread.

Plums

The yellow ones
resemble only themselves,

can be held in one fist
four at a time.

But night one dreams a choir
overflowing with yellow notes,

descending but never quite reaching
the exposed heads of petitioners below.

The color falls
so heavily on the red

ones it bruises.
The purple are still hard.

At least we'll know
when they are ripe, what fragrance,

what texture, what light.
And does the time

they carry inside them
ripen the same? The trees

have been hidden
in the stark ditch. The road itself

sinks and springs
carrying churches and swept stores.

One side barley
already cut; the other

is still gold. The corkscrew road
lifts a forest up,

and, perched on the very top,
a town through which one woman

pushes a baby carriage.
At the Slovak border

what can't be fed
gnaws at the bones, oh, yes,

it hurts. The forest
offers temporary cures,

flowers for bronchitis, *divizna* for fever
and flu, chamomile for sleeping, and water running

under roots, the partisans who lived here,
the German baths and skeletons, all of it

belonged to us. We drank,
and it satisfied

for a while. But in my dream,
I am moving like a tongue

through the mouths of the speechless,
I am biting through buckets of unripe plums, one

by one, ruining each of them
because I can't

tell time.

Pomelo with fallen angel

Sealed inside this yellow peel, beneath the heavy
compressed clouds they call white skin, the wings
are bound and pressed. So when she feels the knife
she quivers, when the skin's peeled back, oh ecstasy.
Yet when the wings are lifted out, they're different
than they were before; instead of wind they're filled
with water, sweet and bitter, each feather fitted
to a narrow juice-filled sac.
                              They look like
the hands of an unripe bride, pale from waiting
in the dark, long slender fingers reaching,
ever unmet. Even if they were to dry a little
in the sun, like cicadas falling out before
they grow into their souls, these wings
won't rise—they left in such a rush. And she
has never learned wane and billow, what has tides,
and what a spoon is for. The wet pomelo feathers
wink like the seven hundred eyes of flies
and scatter like dew, and here she is,
opening her mouth.

Making Sense of the Senses

Filled with lust, a woman goes shopping.
      Her desire deepens and wanders far beyond the capacities
of local industries: frivolous pair of shoes, French manicure, jumper cables, butter.

She is trying to make sense of the senses,
      there on the roof of that tropical hut,
on a beach of panting fish.

The gills open,
      you see red suns and white cathedral bones
and organs piping air.

You can measure the distance of musical scores.
      Stick your fingers in and lift it up.
The suns flee to other shores, the tail feebly wags.

Too often, too vividly described
      to be imagined much, everywhere and all at once,
Dein aschenes Haar Sulamith, and all that.

And when you're not so fortunate,
      it happens just to you,
limpid eyes and waiting feet. For three hours

we have been saying index finger down a spine,
      unbutton button, saying nothing.
Under the eaves the wind is trembling.

Under the leaves the bench back vibrates with a voice.
      It's nothing personal. Just a carved-out sound,
a flash of panic as waves squeeze the air, bravado, a tremble of pain.

Rage is an unlettered word,
      the Spartan chorus before rain. Rain is an unlettered word.
Rage is a measuring spoon

spilling over and over
      again. *Sehr geehrte Damen und Herren*:
When I find a way off this map, it won't be me paying your taxes

and wearing your imported
      Italian shoes. *Mit freundlichen Grüßen*
Lust is a pocketknife too small for the task at hand.

Lust is an unlettered word.
      Rain is a measure of character.
And who can tell her what the peasants ate, and what their surnames are,

and if they slept with the windows open,
      and what they hear through train-shook shades,
and what smells from their garbage pails, and if it tasted good?

Anorexia, with Chorus

When I lay my frame across
your flesh
your belly buoys me
through night,

O red beet of winter, yogurt of despair
sleepy onion eyes of hope
glowing just below.

Timidly your sleeping folds
whisper secrets
of your household,

O urgent avocado
docile mango on its side
little curls of shrimp.

From your ropey scars and sagged
stretch marks
rhythmically are dangling

a girl's chaste breasts
a navel.
Consider the cheeks,

Mixed vixens
viturperative twaddle of peas
and all the skins and leaves.

Consider the raggy cabbage
the silt of mushroom gills
the diasporic cauliflower,

it is not given
to each of us
to be desired.

Cabbage, a Love Song

I dislike you, cabbage. Your tight-fisted order
yielding to my little knives with your
immaculate squeaks. Your rotund indifference to all
that falls away. The fact you feed me through the winter,
through the centuries, and I dislike my need,
the shadows of my lifting fingers cast by your
green light, and all my old sorrow. I dislike
your density, as if the world lacked space, your pure
white heart that open fields can't heat, the way
you fall apart when cooked. You're such a poor loser.
Plus it takes so very long to finish all of you.
I can say without reservation, I hate
all the casual ways you're so unseemly chaste,
so haughty in your modesty, so moderately good.

Rubens' House

Rubens slept in a wooden cabinet,
as did Van Dyck, as did Van Gogh,
on a mattress too short for his full length,
his head and shoulders propped with cushions.
And should the angel of death approach
his couch at night,
                        he could present her
with a plum or fig, translucent fruit,
glowing from beneath his head, plucked
from his garden, or some sweet herbs
from a labyrinth of scent. In his garden,
his grape arbor, his lush lawn,
his house of stone,
                        he could count up
all he had. He could put flesh on a model,
give her lavish furs and robes;
he could fill her mouth with fruit;
he could ring
                    her arms with bands,
her waist with golden coils;
 he could circle her himself,
then count all that he had.
He lacked nothing
                    he would find;
he lacked nothing that he had.
If the gleam of an exotic eye
was like a grape that taunted him
from its curling, draping vines,
he could hold it on his brush,
stroke it onto canvass
                    to contemplate

it at his leisure with a glass of wine.
If its essence slipped away,
he could hold it in his teeth
with the oysters on his plate until
they gleamed, dainty with happiness.

A Travelogue

Grasshoppers and Agave
Monterrey, Mexico

No, it's butter for agave, tender
between the teeth. Whoever professes to hate worms, let him regard
the distorted line in mescal, the plump
shock on cast iron.

Yes, and for the
           grasshopper
olive oil.
      And salt.
             Green and violet
smokey legs
      kick your belly
dreams.

Squid
Kobe, Japan

On the milky plate
a tentacle lies cringing.
Snap. The scissors shut.

Ants and Yucca
Paraitepuy, Venezuela

We eat them before they eat us
says the man who stirs the pot
seasoned hot with venom.
The wet wings undulate above
the broken exoskeletons of ants.
The yucca bob like bare breasts.
The people have few teeth.   They say
their girlfriends knocked them out
in fits. It is bitter, bitter.
A nursing baby whimpers once.

To make fermented *padzáoru*
the women meet and chew
the yucca roots they grew, then spit
them in a trough The pink
is sweeter, the yellow more potent.   ·
You'll dream of the mountain
Roraima, the Mother of Waters,
you'll dream of fruit, of wifeless men
crying on the Kukénam.

Coffee
Zlín, Czech Republic

The grinds cast their fortunes
through your teeth.
If you aren't careful,
if you smile,
the neighbors
will be able to tell
everything about you.

Vegetables
Hiroshima, Japan

Hersey says pumpkins
roasted on the vine. Flowers
bloomed in strange warmth. Red
potatoes baked. Who
placed vases, laid plates?

The History of the Radish

In its wild state it's utterly unknown,
but it may come from China or Japan
and may descend from *Raphanus Raphan-
istrum.* In days of Pharaohs, it was grown
extensively in Egypt. How its name,
from Saxon, *rude, rudo,* or *reod,*
or from the Sanskrit *rudhira,* for blood,
was hid from Britain till Gerard would claim
in 1597, four distinct
varieties. From cellophane, denude
of greeny tops, or peasant fingers, rude
and cakey earth, we lift them to the sink,
recalling how Egyptian women dyed
their nipples scarlet in a braver night.

Goodbye

Ahoj

Goodbye green-eyed name.
Goodbye Vltava with your seven swans

and watery onion bulbs of light.
Goodbye bitten cigarette,

sparks and dewy stars
and smoke from the theatre above the Vltava.

"We are not very brave a people," Milán said. That maybe true,
but they can certainly do *Mephistopheles* in style.

Goodbye, Mephistopheles!
Goodbye, Milán!

Tschüß

Your shadows and your teeth
your coffee pot
your dish of salt
your cutting board
your little spoons
your soap-spotted mirror
your long eyelashes
your dictionaries
and your bicycle your ears
your black leather belt
your creaking floor boards
the corner behind your door
your sheets your cherry tree
your windows your glasses
your newspapers your small
change. Your
Heidegger and Benjamin
your bony hips your chest
of drawers your door hinges
your brushed shoes
your cigarettes your pockets
your keys and
your locks.

Au revoir

Let us leap like gazelles after hunting season
through the paintings of Rousseau.

Let the peach and pear and plum
put forth their incomparable blossoms

and beg and juggle and trick our eyes
in the Place Georges Pompidou.

Let the skeletal mechanisms of water
wash the parted lips of Igor Stravinsky's Place.

O my love, what the mud sucks on your heel
do not track onto my mother's kitchen floor.

Do not stir up le Défenseur de Temps
nor the scarlet ants, their flash of brilliant pain.

Let us roll the voices from our mouths
without thinking about it much.

For your voice is sweet

II

Immigration Quotas

Yam

The first yam's like a finger, fleshy and long,
probing the heat and depth of earth to see what crowns.
The second yam's an umbilical cord between the sky
and the kicking curves of earth. That's why
Yoruba smear cooked yams on rocks and knolls:
we thank the tearful skies, we thank the busty hills,
reconcile your differences, give rain that yams may grow.
Each yam has its own character and use. *Laabako,*
you are first: may no one eat before you,
may no one die from greed; from greed may no
one kill. If there are no *baayeri* in a field
the other yams will leave, but too many *baayeri* will lead
the other yams astray. The little *kpuringa* satisfies
children at play, but at the end of someone's life
chenchito served at burials comforts the tongue
while hands pound out the absent heartbeat on a drum.

Comforts of Home

When I buy vegetables I prefer
to be in my country rather than yours
though in my country crescent moon carrots, radish hearts
are not so juicy and fancifully shaped.

But I prefer to find you in a place
where your vocabulary carves a secret door
through which I can enter or escape.
Where syntax is not a floodlight on my blinded tongue
negotiating taxis at night.

I prefer to be here, where I don't have to lie,
to say I'm married and my man's
the jealous type. He's with the police,
and my father is the ambassador.
Here I am not a bare field in need of a flag.

Here the way I hold tomatoes, touch a cantaloupe
is just like all the others do
and it is your fingers which are different.
You don't watch me carry my purchases home.
I can stare back. And when I smile
it means whatever I want it to.

Unsettled Land Between

I've been thinking about the death of Garcia Lorca,
the Andalusia sun and shadows caging skin,
the inclination to give away what someone comes
to take, and how the difference between the two
is only a matter of time.
                    There the feet of mountains
kick away the sea, but at Coney Island it was all piss
and vomiting.
                    I've been thinking about all the little machines
that make the world work, half-life and shelf-life, closing time.
Museums, newspapers and warranties, those things
that stop time.
                    And what makes it flow—
the shimmer of a spider web and Isadora Duncan's
scarves. How Lorca filled the rift between
one motion and the next
                         with the un-conjugated verb,
how his premonitions were a bridge
more real than what it connected.
Some stand still and some blow up trains and some
poison bread, and this is called
disruption.
                    And that the most common
form of suicide in docile lands today
is the one that causes the most inconvenience
to the greatest number of subway passengers.
Even now the train
                         is backing away from a body. The difference
between a rupture and a rapture, the way gunpowder
is compressed, and how it explodes. And to kiss
well you must know how to leave

                              so that you can learn to enter
an uncommon time—not one, not another,
but its unsettled land between. And how
this is only one kind of answer, one kind of bridge,
and so much depends upon
                              the way the eyes shift,
what a soldier remembers
after the firing squad has scattered.

Field Guide to Silence

He was dusting her silence for fingerprints.
She was taking him out of context.

If words carry with them the traces they have been
so be it.

He was traipsing around in his Armani verbs,
his Cuban-heeled demeanor.

She was always confusing
personification with personality.

Sometimes she thinks Witold Gombrowic
was right about Bruno Schulz.

Too nearing each other they turned around
dumb with yearning.

If he likes metaphors so much
let him make a home in them and be comfortable.

In Peru there are symbols for every thing.
There is a theatre of clouds, there are actors on the mountains.

She bit the hand that feeds her
to see how it would taste.

Central Park

The important thing is to be burdened with your emptiness
—not as a pregnant woman balancing across the street,
for your emptiness belongs only to you and no one
placed it there. Nor are you like a barrel of rainwater

collecting ripples and images. Nor are you a shadow
or a sun. The necessary thing when you
are standing still is to have a place to go. To have something
that should be done or could be done

or at least begun. Consider when your hands
are gathering up strange letters—and they are prone
to slide—they are not grains or seed or keys to a mystery,
though they are not yours, or to a house or a heart.

Bells are not syllables; slaps are not chrysanthemums.
Dictionaries will give you nothing. There is no language
in your blood, no hurt under your boot heels.
What is gliding on the lake is gliding away,

it is looking for fish and frogs. It cannot speak
to you, nor can the oak that drops its button acorns
and moves its arms in the wind. And the children
walking hand in hand before you in the reeds

are only going home to supper. The sun
is setting. It is only the end of the day.
To remember: it's better not to look for things
or pick them up. Stay out of libraries and away

from electrical outlets, hospital rooms and theatres,
from secretaries, businessmen and all who traffic
in similes, stock, grain, meat, desire, daisies
snails and shipping. Stay out of suitcases,

closets, diaries, milk pails, washing machines.
Beware of stockroom boys, of grandmothers
with their heavy tablets of bread, bakers and their ilk.
And yet, it isn't good to be alone. Not too much alone.

The History of Watermelon

Imagine a desert, with real sand, with cracked stones
the color of furnaces, ash-rimmed and glowing
with heat—not an analogy for your own
barrenness—this is a desert. The black granite groans
in the fissures of daybreak, your dry thirsty tongue
stumbles upon a band of nomadic syllables. Here are
the dust-covered hoof prints of livestock, the lizards
that thrive in the shadows, the wind driving forward, the sun. It
is tomorrow or last year or eight thousand years
ago. Time doesn't matter, before you, a tawny
vine languidly stretches as if it were yawning,
the wind parts her leaves, then one hundred melons appear
warm to the touch. Broken open, the pale wet mouths spill
their sweet water, crisp water—now drink your fill.

I Love You Best

Of all the things that don't exist
I love you best, my Herculean mythmaker, my wee god.

In the sea four naked girls, a flat stone I wear over my heart,
and all the while Penelope unravels a shroud.

In the wall beneath the Ukrainian work boots
bricks break and fall:

"That is not art," said the museum guard,
curtly closing the curtains.

Oh, I desire. Yes. Not just firemen and pilots and police,
not just the uniform, but the form itself.

Pain is the failure of reason.
This is a hollow full of rain.

Simone, our timing is off. Just when the body looses its truth
I become most hungry for you.

Tell me about the emptying out of desire,
the gas chamber of the ego.

Undo the shadows, undo the moon,
the plum picker's granddaughter is glistening.

Immigration Quotas

All my life I have been meeting foreigners with green cards. They ride bicycles they cook delicious they buy tickets to the opera they pronounce my name in burning vowels direct my steps with eloquent turns of wrist. But though they have gardens and have set my bones and I have met their great aunts and seen their sofas and smelled their skin they will leave me motionless after sunset the credits picking raspberries the Van Gogh before half-closed eyes of Russian icons and gold leaf glittering under buzzing lights and temperature. The visa will expire too loud to resist the band will hit a wrong note the bank will fail the hand will drop off the shoulder. It will have been vacation high tide an accident a mispronunciation an unfortunate choice an ill-advised use of slang.

Elegy for Arturo Puente

The brother wants to drop out of fifth grade
now Arturo's gone. He's remembering
the fisherman speared by a marlin leaping
across the boat's stern and wants a manly job.

But Aurelia, the eldest, says no; tells him
just thinking is dangerous sometimes, too,
like that Greek guy we read about in school—
an eagle dropped a tortoise on his bald head,

which, from a distance, looked exactly
like a stone. Arturo's death was simple,
almost as if nothing happened at all: The car
fell from its jack in Peterson's Garage.

A sentence so lucid you can't take it
any other way. There must have been
a sharp *boom*, the clatter of the jack
striking the cement, and, much quieter,

the socket wrench dropping from
Arturo's hand. After the funeral the clods
of earth scatter, arch, and fall unseen on
the casket below. If his mother, his five sisters,

balanced on thin, fuzzy legs, had any sort
of premonition the night before he died
they didn't say. My friend Isela always
dreams the soon-to-be deceased's pulling

flowers from a garden. And when my grandfather
died he arrived in his white-and-blue pajamas and
brown house shoes to tell me so himself.
The mourners bite into their German chocolate

cake, clutching white paper plates. The ivy
pulls like fingers on the cemetery fence.
What will they do now, we say. The syllables
of Arturo Puente's name, etched into the breath

of the town, slowly begin to fill with
other conversation, the elements begin to lap
the letters on the headstone so they are drifting with dust
over the garages of minimum wage, with pollen

over fruit trees and grain, across the Texas
coast, over the grazing cows to the west, over
the border. The sisters marry, perhaps a little
sooner than they would have otherwise. More

men part the ribs of a fence and squeeze
through. No one believes in victim of
circumstance. Sometimes the rushing coastal wind
stills suddenly, as if the earth had stumbled.

What the Immigrant Said

The man who brought us to this place
laid his bones down in the field
and dragged a stone over his head.

It is not our home
though we don't remember any other.
These are not our words
though our faces mouth them.

The land that sang in circulars,
brochures, Sudeten newspapers
sputters now with locusts.

But sometimes on the edge of morning
before the shopkeeper shakes me
and the hearth fire wedges its light
under my door, and table and chair
are disentangled from night,

my sleeping muscles twitch as if
this were the day
the earth that breaks
into pieces in the sun
would break for me, too,

and my fences would run like water
to the end of the horizon
and dirt would run like time
through the blades of my plough.

What the Immigrant Said

This pickup truck is so small
I'm sitting in a glass egg,
the windows wet with stars and sweat.

Geese are nesting in the fields.
A hand against my naked breast—
feel stiff wings poised for flight.
Something frightens here.

Bones sink slowly in the earth, heifers
grow fat and conceive. The first tear in every dress,
endangers the virginal seam. Wrinkles, furrows,
painful roots. It's what happens to mother and home.

Nights I am drawn to reluctant fields,
afraid of the movement of stars, gecko feet
on the screen, mouths folding burnt-out moth wings.

Stray Dog in Paradise

She curls up on herself like a hose when she's beat,
and she runs when she's shot with a water stream,
rocks make her wag her tail. She's still young and she
didn't know the kitten's neck would break and she
hates it when the children scream. In her skinny ribs
she hopes. And they're too afraid to keep her,
and they're too sick again to beat her and they haven't got the heart
to see her starve. And the clouds are anviling out,
and the clouds are billowing over, and the young husband
hasn't gotten home.
             Beyond the window can be seen
a little boy blowing on crawling bees. They made
their home in the tree when it was alive. The county's
dredged the river and the cypress knees are starting
to push up through the mud. And because it's just October
the fields are lazy with yellow sprays and the air smells
like mushrooms in the diminishing heat.
             The Zalmans have surveyed
the hundred and forty with global positioning systems
flashing satellites close to Venus at dawn. The dirt
will be moved on Saturday if it doesn't rain.
             Along the road
tiny cotton leaves are pushing through leftover pools of white,
spread like the grandma's hair against her cold potato cheeks,
she slept all through the day and into night.
             And the late
locusts are humming with a Bela Lugosi tone. You can see
on the horizon the sick orange glow of town
like the start of something fainting. It's intangibly appealing
but you've bitten off with bitterness and you've ungraciously
spat and your jealousy runs deeper than you know.

You hope you've not been improvident in your
choice of rootholds.
                    There's a bounty on the ears
of coyotes, fifteen dollars. The homesick young bull
breaks the fence again and again. Across the farm-to-market
road 647 East the neighbors have given their cow pens over
to vines and tangle-weed. Everything grows like mad here
and it's hardly surprising the rate of decay, the stench of
the road, the tranquil smell of manure.
                                    The rifle
lies exhausted by the air compressor coils and the shovel
in your hands is sticking out a lethal tongue. The babies
are sleeping and the moon is slowly rising and the
clouds are parting silver and the dog is gone for now.

Arabella Gets Struck by Lightning

Stubborn clouds had clenched themselves for months, suddenly dropping rain like cows kicking over full buckets of milk.

On the second day the distance between clouds and the sinking earth collapsed, thunder cracked the air as if it were a dish and Arabella crumpled beneath the trees.

She would have calved in six months, so the children begged their father to haul her corpse somewhere they could find it when she became

another white frame drying in the pasture, the baby's shell they imagined curled in her ribs like a ship in a bottle, or like

the double-shelled egg that killed the hen the year before.

It Was Already March

Between November and February
on Farm-to-Market Road 647
East
      you can almost overlook
the fuzz of live-oaks at the distant
ends of ploughed fields so that
the horizon seems infinitely
farther
      almost you could stretch
across the continuum of gray
to Ganado just because you can
see that far
           as if you could step
once into a finger of dust
into the breathless space between
the field and sky so that when the
car once stopped beside your bike
            and you
stopped because you thought he
needed to ask you about a turn
in one of the back roads, or tell you
something about your homework,
it was already March, and
there was nothing you could do
to make it not have happened.

Barbed Wire

Stretching a barbed wire fence across the middle of the field
makes the grass grow greener on both sides.

The new bull rises hot and blank. The ground awaits the hoof prints
of his dynasties; he joins the empty cows.

In the creek a snake uncoils, aims his tuning tongue,
minnows pucker the surface skein of stillness. Anything is possible.

Wire snarls then we snap it tight between us, my brother and me.
We shift balance, punctuate sentences. You want it tight,

but with a little give. Barbs don't know how deep they cut.
Cows are selective eaters when given a choice. But they have no capacity

for planning in winter. We like to minimize decisions
when udders are filling for the first time, teats extending to the hand,

the slobbering mouths of eager calves. The cow and calf know
each other by scent, while everything is separating

into roots and stems, one side of the fence and another.
The newly created cells inside the first-time womb

will split into four stomachs, the liver, tongue
and then gather back into a sausage casing

one sad day of butchering. Our fingers rest briefly
on taut wire, doves scatter, a shot echoes once, for it is hunting season.

What we always wanted most, that which we never knew we had
is in this moment ours, now while the fork is empty,

the lid won't twist off the pickle jar. Where are the fireflies?
Where is the future that stretched like uncoiled wire,

like rolls of butcher paper, beneath fresh meat?

Blemish

If the horizon marks the place
beyond which we can neither see
nor imagine, and you,

a dark dot in the middle,
or perhaps in the upper left-hand corner,
wearing shoes, or barefoot

with the shoes in your hand,
having just removed them
to walk in the sand,

or having just decided to put them on,
do you look up, or out, or
not at all, or in?

Maybe something's
there, and maybe it isn't. It's the form
emptiness spills over, the rim of you,

everything—the shoreline,
the distance, the footprints—
elastic with longing.

Let us praise Braque,
who tried to paint the sensation
of moving around objects,

the feeing of the terrain,
the distances between things.
When a plain meets the sky, you

may be walking on the beach,
still you may be the blemish
on a horizon that won't ripen,

holding the place from which one lifts,
momentarily given,
momentarily borne, and borne again

and given, and given away, and mercifully,
utterly, and yes, let it
be nothing, let it be

at last.

Notes

"An Olive, A Letter"
borrows from sources documenting the outbreak of multiple messianic movements begun by prepubescent girls in Portugal in the 16th Century, during the time of the Inquisition. The visions and activities cited herein are factual. The girls (aged 14-16) were later burned at the stake in the Portuguese Inquisition. The Portuguese Inquisition was established in 1536 to fulfill Manuel I's promise to Maria of Aragon upon their marriage. Most of the victims were the Jews who had fled to Portugal after the 1492 expulsion from Spain and had converted to Catholicism under duress, but who had continued to practice Judaism in secret. Fonseca was a converso, not a leader of a messianic movement, who was married to a wealthy surgeon. She was burned at the stake, as well.

"Plums"
Valassko is a region in Moravia near the Slovak border known for its partisan (or resistance) activity during WWII. *Divizna* is the Czech name for the *Verbascum thapsiforme*, or mullein, which grows wild in the region and is harvested for its curative properties.

"Making Sense of the Senses"
Dien aschenes Haar Sulamith is a line from Paul Celan's *Todesfuge*.

"I Love You Best" refers to Simone Weil.

"What the Immigrant Said"
The state of Texas advertised heavily in the central Europe in the nineteenth century to attract "white" families to replace the *Tejanos*, former citizens of Mexicans who lived in Texas, many of who fought on the side of Texas during the war for independence from Mexico. Originally the wealthiest residents, who occupied the highest social positions, the *Tejanos* were later subject to discrimination and theft of land and commercial property.

"A Girl foresees her future"
The Golden Crescent is a nickname for the Texas Gulf Coast.

Acknowledgements

Some of the poems in this collections, or versions thereof, first appeared in the following journals.

Beltway: "Rubens' House."

The Bend: "Blemish."

Borderlands: Texas Poetry Review: "Making Sense of the Senses" and "What the Immigrant Said."

Drunken Boat: "The Ninth Floor in Caracas," "Yam."

Fence: "A Travelogue," "An Olive, A Letter," and "It was already March."

Greenfuse: "Arabella gets struck by lightning."

Harpur Palate: "Anorexia, With Chorus."

Indiana Review: "A Girl Foresees Her Future."

No Tell Motel: "Field Guide to Silence," "Avocado," "Cabbage," "I Love You Best," and "Immigration Quotas"

The Notre Dame Review: "Exiting Central Park," and "The Comforts of Home."

Quarterly West: "Plums."

River Styx: "The History of the Radish," "The History of Brussels Sprouts."

Spoon River Review. "Falling Fruit."

Third Coast: "The Unsettled Land Between" and "I Love You Best."

"Comforts of Home" has been reprinted in *The Notre Dame Review Ten Year Anthology* and in *Notre Dame Review. The First Ten Years.* Ed. John Matthias and William O'Rourke. South Bend, IN: University of Notre Dame Press, 2009.

A special thanks to David Wevil, Khaled Mattawa, Kim Roberts, Brandel France de Bravo, Sonia Gernes, John Matthias, and Anne Marie Macari. And thanks to Amalia Sulak for her infinite patience.

Marcela Malek Sulak is the author of the poetry chapbook *Of All the Things That Don't Exist, I Love You Best* (Finishing Line Press, 2008). She has translated three book-length collections of poetry, Karel Hynek Macha's *May* and Karel Jaromir Erben's *Bouquet,* from the Czech (Twisted Spoon Press, 1005 & forthcoming in 2010) and Mutombo Nkulu-N'Sengha's Bela-Wenda, from the French (Host Publications, forthcoming in 2010). Her poetry has recently appeared in such journals as *Fence, The Indiana Review, Drunken Boat, River Styx* and *The Notre Dame Review.* She has lived and worked as a free-lance writer and instructor in Germany, the Czech Republic, Venezuela and Israel. This year she is leaving her position as Assistant Professor of Literature at The American University in Washington, DC to direct the Shaindy Rudoff Graduate Program in Creative Writing at Bar-Ilan University.